BE A LEADER

LEADERSHIP ON THE PLAYGROUND

BY JAMES HANCOCK

BLUE OWL
BOOKS

TIPS FOR CAREGIVERS

Leadership can be an intimidating and abstract concept. Finding ways to encourage small, everyday examples of leadership can help instill the traits of a good leader in young readers. It is important to know that there are many leadership traits, forms of leadership, and types of leaders. By helping young people identify all of the possibilities, you can help them find which types of leaders they want to be. Learning how to demonstrate the traits of a leader is a form of social and emotional learning (SEL).

BEFORE READING

Talk to the reader about leadership.

Discuss: What does leadership mean to you?
Who are some leaders in your life? How do they lead?

AFTER READING

Talk to the reader about how he or she can practice leadership.

Discuss: How can you show leadership on the playground?
What traits will you show?

SEL GOAL

Young readers may have a hard time seeing themselves as leaders. Lead a discussion and give examples for inclusion, compassion, and compromise. Use leadership vocabulary. Help readers start to identify leadership traits in themselves. Introduce specific ideas about how to apply these traits on the playground.

TABLE OF CONTENTS

CHAPTER 1

WHAT IS LEADERSHIP?

Ash sees Callie get pushed on the playground. She asks her if she's OK. She helps her up and invites her to play.

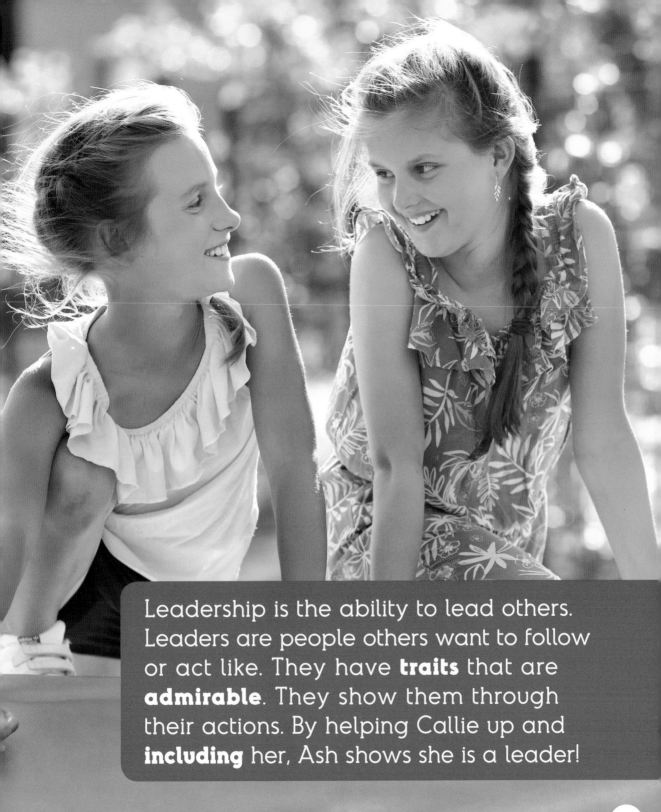

Leadership is the ability to lead others. Leaders are people others want to follow or act like. They have **traits** that are **admirable**. They show them through their actions. By helping Callie up and **including** her, Ash shows she is a leader!

recess monitor

There are many types of leaders. Leaders on the playground can be parents, teachers, or any trusted adults. Trusted adults help solve **conflicts**. Recess monitors help keep everyone safe.

You can lead, too! You don't have to be an adult. Mike is a line leader. He is trusted with **responsibility**. He shows that keeping others safe is important to him.

LEAD AT ANY AGE

You can be a leader at any age! Guiding younger kids is a great way to use your leadership skills. Teach them games. Help them stay safe. You can help lead older kids, too. You could even lead adults!

CHAPTER 2

LEAD WITH COMPASSION

Leaders show **compassion**. Nell sees someone sitting alone on the playground. She looks sad. Nell goes to sit with her. She asks what is wrong and if she can help. She finds out that her new friend's feelings were hurt. Nell tells her a joke to cheer her up. They play together!

A boy falls off of his swing. You don't know him, but you help him to a bench. You find a trusted adult and sit with him until he's ready to play again.

Eve starts a new game. She notices someone playing by herself. She asks her to join the game. Eve makes her feel included. She feels good, too! She made a new friend.

INVITE OTHERS

Sometimes people are afraid to ask to join in. You can ask! If they say no, that's OK. By inviting them, they feel welcome and included anyway! Maybe they will want to play next time.

CHAPTER 3

LEADERSHIP IN ACTION

When you show your leadership skills, you set an example for others to follow. You **inspire** others on the playground to be compassionate, too! That is the power of good leadership.

Being a leader takes **patience**. There will be times when people might not follow you. Or it takes a long time to help friends solve a conflict. Don't give up. Stick with it!

Conflicts happen. There is a disagreement about the game rules. Matt helps find a **compromise**. How? He helps both teams understand each other. First, he finds out what they're disagreeing about. Then he asks what they both want. He comes up with a plan to give both teams some of what they want.

COMPROMISE IN SPORTS

Compromise happens in many sports. In soccer, the winner of the coin toss often gets to choose if his or her team will start with the ball or not. If they choose to start with the ball, the other team gets to choose which side of the field to start on.

Leaders aren't always outgoing. Sam leads by listening. Craig came up with a new game to play. He tells Sam about it.

Sam shows he is listening by nodding his head. He asks a thoughtful question after his friend speaks. He asks what the rules are and when they can play! This helps Craig feel heard. He feels **supported** and **confident**.

Being a leader isn't always easy! But it is **rewarding**. You can help everyone have fun on the playground. You can make new friends! You will feel more confident. Others will, too! How can you be a leader on the playground?

GOALS AND TOOLS

GROW WITH GOALS

Everyone can be a leader on the playground! Build your leadership skills while helping everyone have fun on the playground.

Goal: Invite someone to join you and your friends. Can you include someone new each day?

Goal: Think about how others are feeling on the playground. Show compassion! Comfort someone who is sad. Listen to someone who needs someone to talk to. Can you do this every day for week?

Goal: Next time you see people arguing on the playground, ask if you can help them come up with a compromise. Then help them talk about a solution that includes some of what each person wants. Can you try this once a week?

WRITING REFLECTION

At the beginning of the week, write down 3 categories in a notebook: observations, actions, and goals. Then during the week, watch for examples of people showing leadership on the playground. Write down what they did under "observations." Then think about times that you showed leadership on the playground. Write these under "actions." Finally, make a list of leadership skills you want to try for the next week under "goals."

GLOSSARY

admirable
Deserving praise or admiration.

compassion
A feeling of sympathy for and a desire to help someone who is suffering.

compromise
An agreement that is reached after people with opposing views each give up some of their demands.

confident
Having a strong belief in your own abilities.

conflicts
Serious and usually lengthy disagreements.

including
Welcoming.

inspire
To influence and encourage someone to achieve or do something.

patience
The ability to put up with problems or delays without getting angry or upset.

responsibility
A duty or job.

rewarding
Offering or bringing satisfaction.

supported
Received help, comfort, or encouragement.

traits
Qualities or characteristics that make people different from each other.

TO LEARN MORE

Finding more information is as easy as 1, 2, 3.

1. Go to www.factsurfer.com

2. Enter "**leadershipontheplayground**" into the search box.

3. Choose your cover to see a list of websites.

INDEX

Blue Owl Books are published by Jump!, 5357 Penn Avenue South, Minneapolis, MN 55419, www.jumplibrary.com

Copyright © 2020 Jump! International copyright reserved in all countries. No part of this book may be reproduced in any form without written permission from the publisher.

Library of Congress Cataloging-in-Publication Data

Names: Hancock, James, author.
Title: Leadership on the playground / by James Hancock.
Description: Minneapolis: Jump!, Inc., 2020. | Series: Be a leader | Includes index. | Audience: Ages 7–10
Identifiers: LCCN 2019039903 (print)
LCCN 2019039904 (ebook)
ISBN 9781645272359 (hardcover)
ISBN 9781645272366 (paperback)
ISBN 9781645272373 (ebook)
Subjects: LCSH: Leadership–Juvenile literature. | Playgrounds–Juvenile literature.
Classification: LCC HM1261 .H364 2020 (print)
LCC HM1261 (ebook) | DDC 303.3/4–dc23
LC record available at https://lccn.loc.gov/2019039903
LC ebook record available at https://lccn.loc.gov/2019039904

Editor: Susanne Bushman
Designer: Molly Ballanger

Photo Credits: Pixel-Shot/Shutterstock, cover; Luis Louro/Shutterstock, 1; Veronica Louro/Shutterstock, 3; kiankhoon/iStock, 4; Kamil Macniak/Shutterstock, 5; paylessimages/iStock, 6–7; Wavebreakmedia/iStock, 8–9, 20–21; stockyimages/Shutterstock, 10; Jordan Lye/Getty, 11; martinedoucet/iStock, 12–13; Sergey Novikov/Shutterstock, 14; TinnaPong/Shutterstock, 15; RosalreneBetancourt 13/Alamy, 16–17; CREATISTA/iStock, 18–19.

Printed in the United States of America at Corporate Graphics in North Mankato, Minnesota.